Small Studio • Great Impact

SO1O • 2UO • 3RIO

Edited & published by
Viction:ary

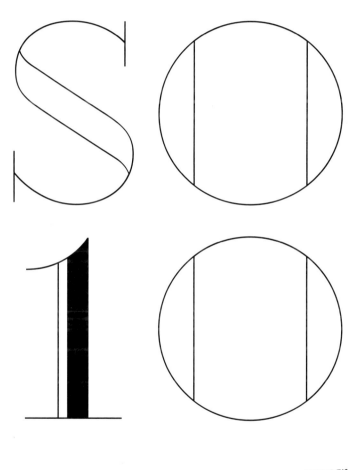

viction:ary

Then & Now.

Like most designers I worked for someone else. I went to work every day, working for 'the man', 'the boss', the person who's 'ball it is'. And that was fine, life was sweet, no stress, then the niggles started. 'I could do this, I could be the boss, I could be 'the man'. Couldn't I?

And so after being 'employed', I found myself one day 'self-employed', sitting in front of my shiny new laptop in a flat in Camden. Life was sweet right? I could do what I wanted, I could take the day off, say no to work I didn't want to do, brilliant.

And so this was how it started. Build was born.

I'm not really a practical person. I can change a light bulb, I can wire a plug if pushed, but run a business? I don't really think I was prepared for that part. The creative? No problem, but run a business — that bit was harder. I was very naive back then, I didn't really pay attention to the business side of things. For me it was all about the work.

The pained artiste doing his thing. 'It's art darling!'.

Wrong.

But I had a secret weapon. Nicola J Place, back then working for Sony PlayStation. Nicky joined the studio full-time in 2006. Working from the dining table in our compact kitchen Nicky brought order from chaos (lesson =1). The studio finally started operating as a business, not just a hobby. For me having someone else as a partner in business was very important (lesson =2). It balanced things out. The studio had different points of view. Its offer was much greater.

The next year saw us move out of the flat and into a studio space. The foundation had been laid over the previous years, contacts had been made, work had been done, this was the dawn of a new era in the history of Build.

Having a dedicated studio meant a great deal to us both. Yes it was scary — our overheads were higher but it made a massive difference in how we ran the business. We could have clients over for meetings, interns in, we worked smarter. But just as important it meant our home and work lives were separated (this is very important).

Now we had the studio and a much better working system (lesson =3), our roles within it defined, our reputation growing, things started to click. Our studio grew organically, we got more clients — this in turn meant that we had more work (great!), but I was at the same time starting to strain in terms of getting the work done. Something had to give. I am a very hands on designer, I enjoy 'doing'. I found it hard to 'share'. This quickly became a problem. We solved this by starting a small programme of internships, as well as hiring freelancers — in other words getting people in and sharing the work and the

studio. From this I learnt to be more 'hands-free', directing people (so that's why it's called a Creative Director). My new found love of sharing, resulted in us finding and eventually employing our first full-time member of staff, designer Joe Luxton (Build employee =001).

Now we were three.

This was another hurdle met and overcome.

Now we had more people in the studio. This meant that we could do more work, take on more clients and hopefully make more money (lesson = 4). It was a big hurdle but to move forwards we had to do it, the studio dynamic changed massively. It was no longer just Nicky and I. Another lesson learned, studio culture is important, input is important. Someone else's view of the world is important (lesson =5), it makes the studio stronger.

Reputation is important, but you can't rely on it forever (lesson =6). We had never done 'new business', business came to us, but this is something that we are having to think about more and more. As designers we are always looking for that bigger job, that project that takes you in a different direction, this takes strategy.

When we started 11 years ago, our strategy consisted of doing great work, and people will come (Genesis 11:1-9 'If you build it, he will come') and to a large extent that hasn't changed. We still want to do great work, for great people. But how we go about that has changed, we've grown up if you like.

The studio has also grown up, we have a new bigger space. Nicky has an assistant, Sophie James (Build employee =002). Now we are four, at our core.

Build turned 11 this year, that's pretty amazing to be still in business given the current climate. We are entrusted with bigger projects, even though we are a small studio, it's still hard work (lesson =7), and it's certainly not glamourous much of the time (lesson =8). But it's all ours, and though it's tough at times, I'm incredibly proud of what we have achieved. We're really excited about our next 11 years, and most importantly how Build will evolve.

Michael C. Place, **Build**

London, UK

Michael C. Place is the creative director and founder of celebrated creative studio, Build, based in East London. The studio has just blown the candles of its 11th birthday in 2012.

Picasso
Guernica
1937

Andrés Soria Olmedo

SONBRUSQUE
MALLORCA

24 DE
JUNIO

HIERBA LUISA

La
innoc

e la
ncia

SONBRUSQUE
MALLORCA

24 DE
JULIO

GUINDILLAS

C O S

CARL SAGAN

M O S

Men
Ro

Arte y
Guerra
Civil

Rocío Robles Tardío

Federico
García Lor
Dibujos
como poem

Picasso
escultor

ASTRID STAVRO STUDIO

Balearic Islands, Spain

Key member / Astrid Stavro
Specialty / Graphic design
URL / www.astridstavro.com

Est. 2004

> "My ambition is to stay small, with the freedom to do the work I like and believe in."

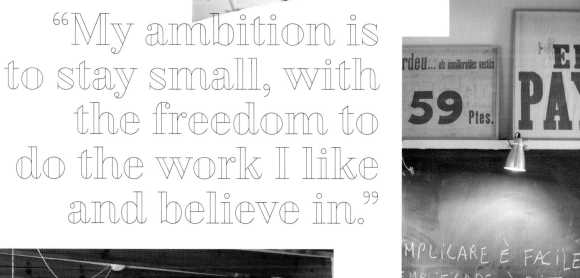

Founded by Astrid Stavro, Astrid Stavro Studio remains consciously small on the Spanish Balearic Islands, offering hands-on intelligent and innovative editorial design solutions like design artisans, to publishing giants like Phaidon Press and independent publishers like Arcadia. Their style is based on clean and distinctive typography with an instantly recognisable style. Stavro is a contributing editor of Elephant magazine and a member of International Society of Typographic Designers (ISTD).

Portrait: Mariano Herrera,
Studio shots: Toni Amengual

5

02

HOW DID YOU START YOUR COMPANY? WHAT IS/ARE YOUR CREED(S) AND ASPIRATION(S)?

I started the company after graduating from The Royal College of Art in 2004. Our ambition is to stay small but still have enough presence in the industry to attract interesting new clients.

The studio is consciously small. We work like design artisans, offering high-quality, hands-on solutions for a select range of clients. We have an international reputation for appropriate and discerning editorial design with a strong emphasis on clean, distinctive and considered typography.

Our underlying principles are clarity, simplicity and commitment to finding unique, tailor-made solutions for each project in a conscious effort to avoid repetition and formulaic responses. Our approach is idea-based and rigorous. We start with extensive research and analysis of the content. Craft and content should work together as a whole. The key is in the process. The dialogue. Asking the right questions and understanding the objectives. "To complicate is easy. To simplify is difficult." — Bruno Munari.

01

WHAT HAS BEEN DIFFICULT FOR YOU AT THE BEGINNING?

At the beginning everything was difficult — from making an invoice to trying to convince clients about a good idea (this is still a very hard part).

WHAT ROLES DO YOU PLAY IN THE FIRM?

I have multiple roles: creative director, art director, designer, accountant and secretary!

HOW DO YOU PROMOTE YOURSELF?

We don't really need self-promotion. Our last promotional mailer was sent five years ago. We use social networks for communicating quickly and cheaply.

WHAT MAKE(S) SMALL STUDIOS SUSTAINABLE? WHAT IS MOST CRITICAL FOR STUDIOS LIKE YOURS TO GAIN A FOOTHOLD IN THE COMPETITIVE MARKET?

Small means less expenses and more freedom to accept or reject specific projects. If you produce great work you will keep on finding work, no matter how small you are. One of the great advantages of being small is to be able to work in a more artisanal, hands-on way. We are involved in every stage of the project, something that doesn't happen in bigger studios or agencies. It also means longer hours and overall it is pretty tough but at the end also very rewarding.

03

04

IT MIGHT BE EASIER FOR LARGE DESIGN AGENCIES TO WIN A JOB. WHAT ARE YOUR STRATEGIES TO BEAT THEM? HAVE YOU EVER LOST HAD TO GIVE UP AN OPPORTUNITY THAT MIGHT BE RELEVANT TO YOUR COMPANY SIZE?

We don't have strategies to 'beat' anyone. We are passionate about our work, so the answer is in the process and keeping things simple. Our clients come to us because they like and understand what we do. Many of them have been working with us for years. If we pitch for bigger projects we sometimes join forces with other creatives and designers.

WHAT ARE THE BEST AND WORST EXPERIENCES BY FAR?

The best: freedom. The worst: stress.

HAVE YOU EVER THOUGHT ABOUT ADDING (A) NEW PARTNER(S) OR HIRING STAFF? WHAT COULD BE A PROBLEM YOU HAVE EVER IMAGINED?

I never thought of adding a new partner but this doesn't mean it might not happen.

I've been hiring staff practically since the first day I opened the studio.

WHAT DO YOU DO WHEN YOU GET BOGGED DOWN AT A JOB?

Go for a walk, a drive, play with my son, read books, anything that is not work!

DO YOU INTEND TO RETAIN YOUR PRACTICE'S CURRENT SIZE? IF IT HAS TO GROW BIG ONE DAY, WHAT WOULD BE THE ULTIMATE SIZE?

I have no intention to grow bigger, on the contrary, my ambition is to stay small.

AND THE TRADITION(S) ETHOS TO KEEP?

The freedom to do the work I like and believe in.

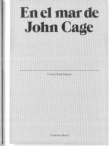

06

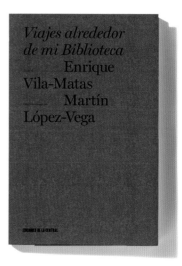

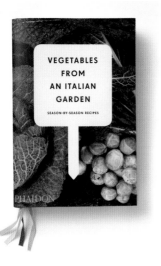

09

10

01 / Mirror of Languages_2008
Exhibition catalogue based on Mercè Rodoreda's novel. Designed with Ana Domínguez. Photos by Mauricio Salinas.

02, 05 / Son Brusque_2011-12
Packaging designed with Pablo Martín.

03 / Syzygy_2008
Poster for a one-day conference, designed with Richard Sarson.

04 / Narrative Collection_2011
Book collection with trimmed covers.

06 / Cuadernos Postal_2009
Monographs on artists and architects introduced as postcard notebooks.

07 / La Librería de los Escritores_2008
New design for Mijaíl Osorguín's literature collection, The Writer's Library.

08 / AGI BCN Congress Guides_2011
Catalogues created with Mario Eskenazi, Patrick Thomas, Pablo Martín. Typeface by Andreu Balius, Alex Trochut.

09 / Vegetables from an Italian Garden_ 2011
Seasonal Italian cooking guide designed with Marianne Noble.

10 / 14x22_2009
Book collection about artist's writings.

Having a penchant for travelling and meeting people, Daniel Brokstad (b.1988) is a young and outgoing graphic designer and photographer, with a knack for identity, packaging and type design. Brokstad studied at RMIT, Melbourne and is currently working full-time as a designer at advertising agency, Procontra, and freelance on the side, in Stavanger, Norway, where he was born.

"Nothing is ever perfect, I always want to learn and become better at what I do."

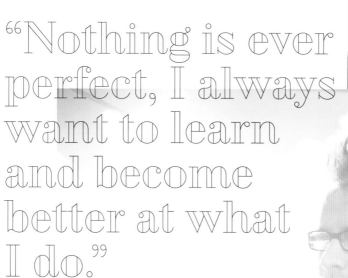

DANIEL BROKSTAD

Stavanger, Norway

....

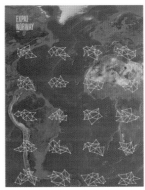

Key member / Daniel Brokstad
Specialties / Graphic design, Photography
URL / www.danielbrokstad.com

....

Est. 2009

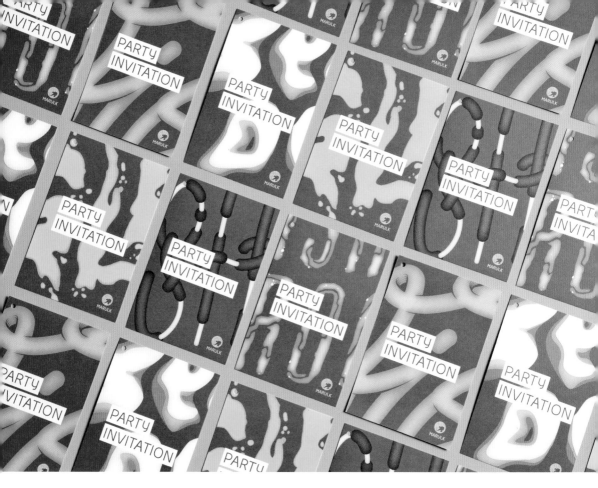

HOW DID YOU START YOUR COMPANY? WHAT IS/ARE YOUR CREED(S) AND ASPIRATION(S)?

I originally started my own business in Australia, back in 2009 while I was in the middle of my communication design studies at RMIT University in Melbourne. In the beginning I was mainly getting different photography jobs, but I eventually started moving more and more over to design. I later continued my business in Norway when I moved back in the spring of 2011.

WHAT HAS BEEN DIFFICULT FOR YOU AT THE BEGINNING?

The most difficult thing in the beginning was obviously getting clients. I didn't know where to start and how to get them. In hindsight I see a lot of things I could have done differently to gain more clients.

WHAT ROLES DO YOU PLAY IN THE FIRM?

I'm a one-man band as a freelancer. So I have both the highest position and the lowest as the same time. Which means it's the best, but I also have to do all the dirty work myself.

01

HOW DO YOU PROMOTE YOURSELF?

Facebook, Twitter, Instagram, Behance, my personal website and of course always handing out business cards as I introduce myself to people. While it's been easier to spread the word of my design online, most of my clients are still met through face-to-face contact or by word of mouth.

WHAT MAKE(S) SMALL STUDIOS SUSTAINABLE? WHAT IS MOST CRITICAL FOR STUDIOS LIKE YOURS TO GAIN A FOOTHOLD IN THE COMPETITIVE MARKET?

I think smaller studios and freelancers have more freedom which in many cases allows them to create designs that might not have been possible through a studio, at least not in a corporate advertising agency. I think this is quite important for smaller studios to get a grip on the market and get a share of the clients, by offering something different from their competitors.

IT MIGHT BE EASIER FOR LARGE DESIGN AGENCIES TO WIN A JOB. WHAT ARE YOUR STRATEGIES TO BEAT THEM? HAVE YOU EVER LOST HAD TO GIVE UP AN OPPORTUNITY THAT MIGHT BE RELEVANT TO YOUR COMPANY SIZE?

My clients are smaller businesses themselves, so I don't really get into any straight competition with the design studios. They have their big clients and I keep my small ones.

WHAT ARE THE BEST AND WORST EXPERIENCES BY FAR?

Worst? I accepted a CD album design job together with a friend from another design studio, but after we already accepted the job, it ended up with a payment that was less than half of what I was told. We were then told they were going to release it on vinyl and, instead of focusing on money, we decided to go all in on the job and just create something really awesome and get a cool vinyl out. Two months later and after 100 hours of work and sketching up different solutions, none of the solutions was approved and the final design was done right before deadline in just one day. The little payment didn't arrive until eight months later.

Best? It's really hard to define the very best experience. There were many great moments but I would say my general good feel about my design comes from people who actually appreciate my design, getting good feedback, being asked to attend exhibitions, publish my work, etc. It lets me know I'm at least doing something right. Design is all about communication, and this is a confirmation that my design communicated to its audience.

HAVE YOU EVER THOUGHT ABOUT ADDING (A) NEW PARTNER(S) OR HIRING STAFF? WHAT COULD BE A PROBLEM YOU HAVE EVER IMAGINED?

Not really, to be honest. Freelance is currently something I'm just doing on the side since I'm employed full-time in a studio.

WHAT DO YOU DO WHEN YOU GET BOGGED DOWN AT A JOB?

There're a few alternatives. One could be to try getting away from the work. Go out, get some fresh air, do something completely different, hang out with friends, have a drink, disconnect. Then later return to the work with a pair of fresh eyes on the situation. A completely different approach is to dig deeper into the work, for example by doing some more research on the client, the theme concept and the client's competitors, or heading over to creative design blogs for inspiration and motivation. Often I will just save and close the document, then start off fresh from the beginning. Either this will create something new and interesting, or make me realise the new direction is a bad idea and that the original idea actually was a good one.

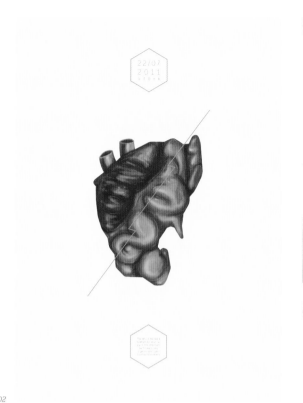

02

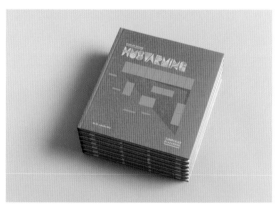

03

04

DO YOU INTEND TO RETAIN YOUR PRACTICE'S CURRENT SIZE? IF IT HAS TO GROW BIG ONE DAY, WHAT WOULD BE THE ULTIMATE SIZE AND THE TRADITION(S) ETHOS TO KEEP?

For now, I will just continue on as a lone wolf. But if I ever was to start my own proper studio with employees, I think the "ultimate size" would be about five to six people. I would want a smaller studio with predominant focus on ideas and execution, and less on administration.

Creativity as the key element without any doubt. Money isn't everything. Secondly, a very relaxing and cool work space. Down to earth, no bureaucracy and hierarchy. A small group working more together as friends instead of pure business partners, but of course still in a professional manner.

05

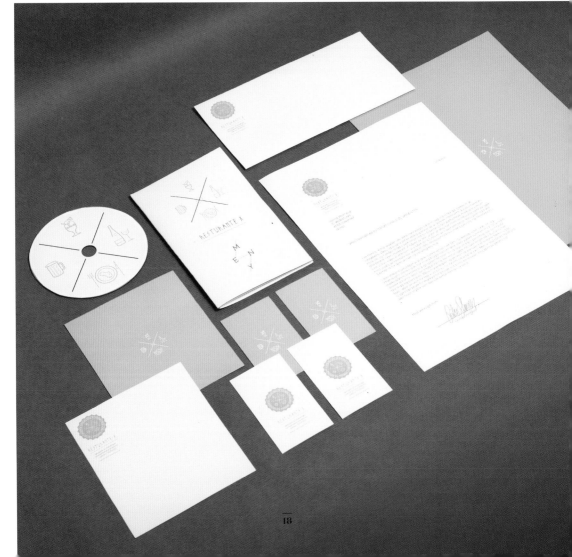

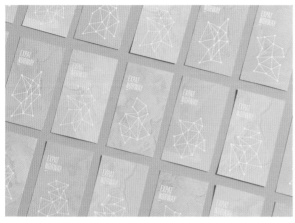

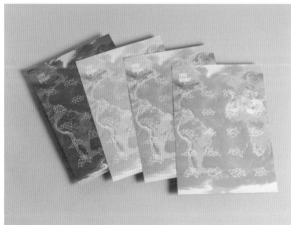

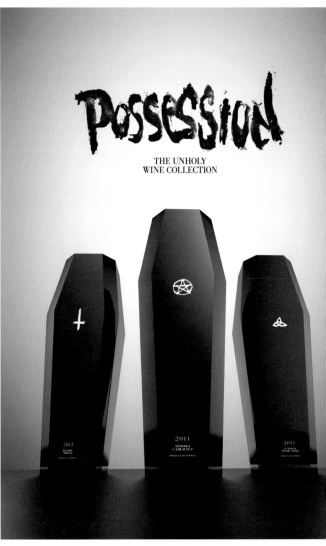

POSSESSION

**THE UNHOLY
WINE COLLECTION**

01 / *Marulk Party_2012*
Invitation to celebrate Eni Norge's start of production at Marulk oil field. Created at Procontra. Art-directed by Jone Johannessen. Text by Morten Aamodt.

02 / *Heart Attack_2011*
Poster design based on the attacks in Norway for Positive Poster.

03 / *Husvarming Book_2012*
"Housewarming" book for a new concert hall's opening. Created at Procontra. Project managed by Marianne Barstad. Art-directed by Anita Brekke. Text by Morten Aamodt.

04 / *Janne Joakim Identity_2011*
Identity for a photographer.

05 / *Resturante X_2011*
Identity for a high-end restaurant.

06 / *Expat Norway_2012*
Identity for a relocation service company in Norway. Created at Procontra. Art-directed by Jone Johannessen. Text by Morten Aamodt.

07 / *Possession_2012*
Packaging for a limited "unholy" wine collection.

08 / *LE PÉCHÉ_2010*
Packaging for a premium absinthe.

08

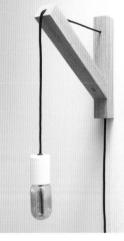

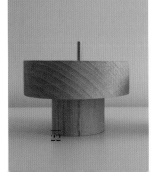

Portrait: Jami Saunders

DINO
SANCHEZ LLC
New York City, NY, USA

Key member / Dino Sanchez
Specialty / Product design
URL / www.dinosanchez.com

Est. 2010

"Anyone can make anything now, so I only focus on making good things."

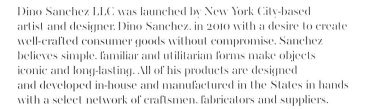

Dino Sanchez LLC was launched by New York City-based
artist and designer, Dino Sanchez, in 2010 with a desire to create
well-crafted consumer goods without compromise. Sanchez
believes simple, familiar and utilitarian forms make objects
iconic and long-lasting. All of his products are designed
and developed in-house and manufactured in the States in hands
with a select network of craftsmen, fabricators and suppliers.

HOW DID YOU START YOUR COMPANY? WHAT IS/ARE YOUR CREED(S) AND ASPIRATION(S)?

I've been designing products on the consulting side for nearly 12 years and while work has been very good for me, it typically comes with compromise. There are quite a few channels that kind of work has to go through before it hits the market, if it hits the market at all.

I started Dino Sanchez LLC with the intent of producing work that I wanted to produce, with little to no compromise.

WHAT HAS BEEN DIFFICULT FOR YOU AT THE BEGINNING?

To achieve that, all the work is designed, developed and fabricated all within a very tight knit group of people here in the US. That being said, it does have its challenges.

WHAT ROLES DO YOU PLAY IN THE FIRM?

I have my hand in pretty much every aspect of the business, from design and development to vendor and retail partnerships. I see every piece that goes out the door.

HOW DO YOU PROMOTE YOURSELF?

There are literally a million channels to get the word out, e.g. blogs, publications, social media. It's really quite simple. However, despite the quantity, there's limited quality. The quality work will find itself with the quality press.

WHAT MAKE(S) SMALL STUDIOS SUSTAINABLE? WHAT IS MOST CRITICAL FOR STUDIOS LIKE YOURS TO GAIN A FOOTHOLD IN THE COMPETITIVE MARKET?

Keeping small is what keeps me sustainable. I'm obviously aware of what's out there, but I don't really think of this as competition. Anyone can make anything now, so I only focus on making good things. The good work will naturally rise to the top and ultimately be the things the market will want.

IT MIGHT BE EASIER FOR LARGE DESIGN AGENCIES TO WIN A JOB. WHAT ARE YOUR STRATEGIES TO BEAT THEM? HAVE YOU EVER LOST/HAD TO GIVE UP AN OPPORTUNITY THAT MIGHT BE RELEVANT TO YOUR COMPANY SIZE?

I don't really see this as competition, but to be honest I don't really feel like we're missing out. If anything, I think the bigger companies are missing out on what we smaller companies are doing. By default we're closer to our work — we have to be and to me that's what makes this all worthwhile. I have an attachment to every piece we produce.

01

02

03

04

WHAT ARE THE BEST AND WORST EXPERIENCES BY FAR?

Best: realising we did something good. Worst: realising we did something not good.

HAVE YOU EVER THOUGHT ABOUT ADDING (A) NEW PARTNER(S) OR HIRING STAFF? WHAT COULD BE A PROBLEM YOU HAVE EVER IMAGINED?

Right now I consider Dino Sanchez LLC as being myself and everyone who has anything to do with the production of my work. I could never do this alone. I have a small network of people I trust and it's been nothing but great working with them.

05

WHAT DO YOU DO WHEN YOU GET BOGGED DOWN AT A JOB?

Since this is a small operation and I have a fair amount of control determining when work gets released. I can afford to stop and do something else. I always have at least 5-10 things going on at once. so if I'm stuck on one thing. I'll go to something else. Things are always in motion. so I start a set of work while another is being produced. I honestly don't have the time to get stuck.

DO YOU INTEND TO RETAIN YOUR PRACTICE'S CURRENT SIZE? IF IT HAS TO GROW BIG ONE DAY. WHAT WOULD BE THE ULTIMATE SIZE AND THE TRADITION(S) ETHOS TO KEEP?

It's difficult to project growth for a small business like mine. It's not something I concern myself with. at least not right now. If there ever comes a time to grow. it can't come at the expense of compromising the quality of the work.

Regardless of size. my ethos towards design has always been to constantly create and try to do good work. I truly believe that's it and so far. so good!

LEAVE THAT SMELL BEHIND
www.keepairfresh.com
2150 / 5000

06

01 / *Totems: Series One_2012*
Stackable wooden blocks handmade
from solid oak.

02 / *Stacks: Lamps_2011*
Desk lamp with birch plywood frame and
ceramic fitting.

03 / *Bracket Lamps_2011*
Lamp with solid oak wall bracket, crafted
and assembled by hand.

04 / *Tumble Lamps_2011*
Lamps turned out of solid ash which can
sit upright or "tumble" on their side.

05 / *Stacks: Speakers_2010*
Prototype speakers designed to overstate
their presence in a cluster of six.

06/ *Keep Air Fresh_2009-12*
Three-year installation campaign for
public restrooms across the U.S.

07 / *Thieves Like Us_2011*
Typographic art project created with
Commercial Type. Photos by Paúl Rivera.

07

DRAWSWORDS
Amsterdam, the Netherlands

Key member / Rob van den Nieuwenhuizen
Specialty / Graphic design
URL / www.drawswords.com

Est. 2008

Amsterdam-based design studio DRAWSWORDS is the brainchild of graphic designer Rob van den Nieuwenhuizen founded in 2008. The studio designs for both cultural and commercial fields and works on projects ranging from visual identities and publications to music packaging and websites. DRAWSWORDS also initiates projects of its own, such as the Langscapes series (2008), which features type-based posters and tracks specially created by several Dutch composers based on given text.

"I always knew I wanted to be my own boss."

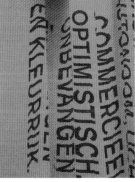
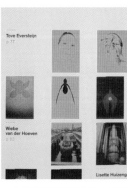

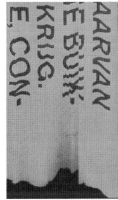

DNK 18

GESLAAGDE
PRESENTATIE KABK TIJDENS
ONTWERP-PLATFORM DESIGN
WHY? IN MILAAN

GROTE
DIVERSITEIT IN
DE EINDVOOR-
STELLINGEN VAN
DE DANSVAK-
OPLEIDING

01

03

HOW DID YOU START YOUR COMPANY? WHAT IS /ARE YOUR CREED(S) AND ASPIRATION(S)?

Coming from an entrepreneurial background (my father started his own company when I was still pretty young). I always knew I wanted to be my own boss. I guess I don't handle authority really well :)

Right after graduation I was asked — together with a classmate — for a one-year job placement at the Royal Academy of Art. During that year we functioned as an in-house but independent design studio without really having to make compromises. That felt so great that I decided to start my own studio.

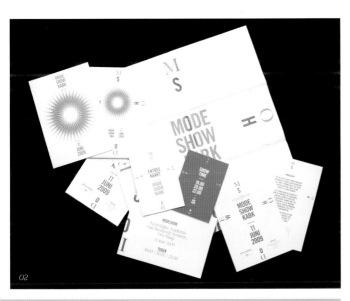

02

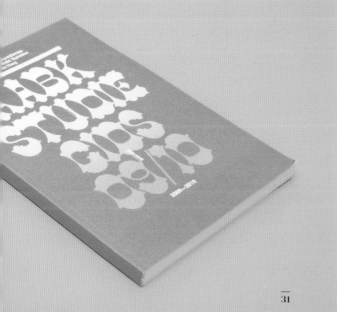

WHAT HAS BEEN DIFFICULT FOR YOU AT THE BEGINNING?

It was and still is particularly difficult to stop working. I work all the time. I don't mind it because I really love what I do but I guess sometimes I need to sit back and relax for a bit.

WHAT ROLES DO YOU PLAY IN THE FIRM?

Since this is a one-man studio: all of them.

HOW DO YOU PROMOTE YOURSELF?

I don't really see it as promoting myself. I'm quite active on Facebook and Twitter and me and my friends also host exhibitions and parties and such at our own ground floor project space. I guess I'm one of those types of people you'll see at a lot of parties, presentations and openings. And just to make myself clear: I go there because I like it and not for the sake of networking :)

WHAT MAKE(S) SMALL STUDIOS SUSTAINABLE? WHAT IS MOST CRITICAL FOR STUDIOS LIKE YOURS TO GAIN A FOOTHOLD IN THE COMPETITIVE MARKET?

Work hard, work smart and do whatever you do as good as possible.

IT MIGHT BE EASIER FOR LARGE DESIGN AGENCIES TO WIN A JOB. WHAT ARE YOUR STRATEGIES TO BEAT THEM? HAVE YOU EVER LOST /HAD TO GIVE UP AN OPPORTUNITY THAT MIGHT BE RELEVANT TO YOUR COMPANY SIZE?

It's impossible to compete with large studios in terms of scale or man hours, but you can of course compete on a conceptual and on a personal level. When I do a project, my commissioner knows it is really me that will pick up the phone, come to the meetings, talk to the printer and do the corrections. I'm far more involved with the projects than any designer working at a large studio.

Just recently me and my friends — we have a design collective called Almanak — lost a huge pitch to a big, famous studio. The client really liked our work and thought we were much more progressive and experimental, but in the end they decided to base their choice on stability and experience. I actually think that's kind of sad, since now it feels their choice was based on fear. It would have been a great statement to pick a smaller studio.

WHAT ARE THE BEST AND WORST EXPERIENCES BY FAR?

Best: meeting lots of nice people and doing awesome projects. Worst: working waaaay too much.

04

ALL THE WAY 1 ○ (3.47)
THE FIX 2 ○ (3.07)
DELIRIUM 3 ○ (...4)
ENLIGHTEN ME 4 ○ (3.26)
SNAKES & LADDERS 5 ○ (3.18)
MOVE ON 6 ○ (...0)

MOVE ON
BURNING BRIDGES 7 ○ (4.51)
DEAD END 8 ○ (2.27)
GUARDIAN 9 ○ (5.11)
PARALUSION 10 ○ (3.12)
THE MAZE 11 ○ (4.45)

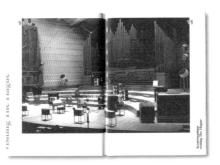

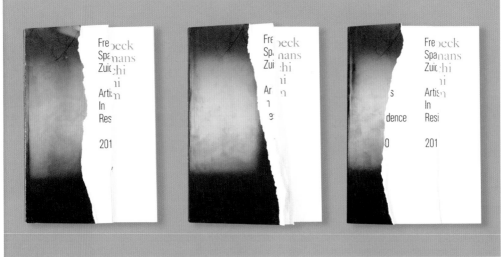

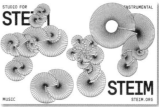

08

HAVE YOU EVER THOUGHT ABOUT ADDING (A) NEW PARTNER(S) OR HIRING STAFF? WHAT COULD BE A PROBLEM YOU HAVE EVER IMAGINED?

Yes I have and that's why we also started a design collective so we can help each other out. Hiring staff would be the next step but right now I feel more comfortable doing it like this.

WHAT DO YOU DO WHEN YOU GET BOGGED DOWN AT A JOB?

Mostly: going to concerts and or playing music myself. Anything music-related actually. Even though I love (graphic) design, music is and will remain the most important thing in my life.

DO YOU INTEND TO RETAIN YOUR PRACTICE'S CURRENT SIZE? IF IT HAS TO GROW BIG ONE DAY, WHAT WOULD BE THE ULTIMATE SIZE AND THE TRADITION(S) ETHOS TO KEEP?

I would love for this studio to grow into something a little bit bigger without becoming too big. I've seen what happens when a company becomes bigger and bigger and I don't really feel like turning into a full-time manager. I want to design stuff and I want to be involved in every single step of a process. But that depends on the size of the projects as well. I guess. Five to ten people seems like a good size. Most of those would be designers or programmers but I guess the addition of one or two project managers would be a smart move :)

I think it's really important to keep on challenging yourself and to really think about what makes you happy. Personally I'm someone who gets bored with stuff very easily, so I'm always trying to improve and I love learning from other people.

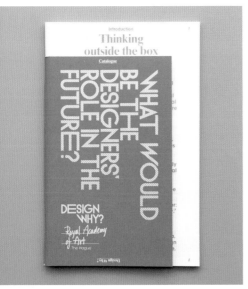

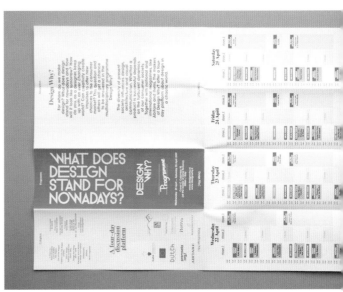

10

01 / De Nieuwe K_2008-09
Quarterly redesigned for Royal Academy of Art, The Hague (KABK), Royal Conservatoire and Leiden University. Created with Mattijs de Wit.

02 / KABK Fashion Show_2009
KABK annual graduation show identity. Created with Mattijs de Wit.

03 / KABK Guide_2009
Study guide design.

04 / Face Tomorrow_2011
Packaging for a Dutch indie band's namesake album. Created with Barbara Hennequin.

05 / Fail Again Fail Better #2_2009
Collateral for an exhibition in MKgalerie Rotterdam and Berlin.

06 / Acousmonium_2008
Programme for Groupe de Recherches Musicales' Acousmonium orchestra.

07 / Intimate Stories on Absence_2010
Catalogue published after a one-year residency program. Created with Remco van Bladel.

08 / STEIM_2011-12
Identity and collateral for an independent music centre. Produced with Remco van Bladel and Micha Bakker.

09 / Design Why?_2009
Identity and catalogue for Design Why? exhibition during Il Salone del Mobile 2009. Created with Mattijs de Wit.

10 / Open Day KABK_2009
KABK open day identity. Created with Mattijs de Wit.

"For me, it's all about the work."

JAMIE MITCHELL
Sydney, Australia

Key member / Jamie Mitchell
Specialty / Art direction
URL / www.jamiemitchell.nl

Est. 2002

Having been in the field for more than ten years, Jamie Mitchell is an Australian-born art director greatly influenced by Dutch design, present in his work spanning advertising, packaging, environmental design. Prior to running his own firm, he was an art director at BBC (London), Me Company (London) and Dietwee (Amsterdam). Mitchell has now returned to Australia with experience working with prominent clients, inclusive of Anton Corbijn, Nike, Vogue and MTV.

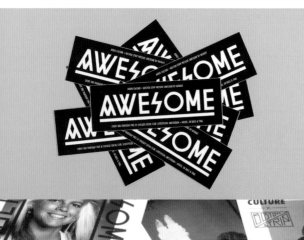

01

HOW DID YOU START YOUR COMPANY? WHAT IS/ARE YOUR CREED(S) AND ASPIRATION(S)?

I started my own company in 2002. I aim to create visually powerful communication that always has something to say.

Dutch design has played a big part in this. Its directness and bold expression can clearly be seen in my work, to which I've added my own personality and high level of craftsmanship. This results in a design approach that's proven to add value to both products and companies. I apply this approach across all areas of communication, from advertising, packaging and retail to environmental, interior and graphic design. And work with clients to combine these into the most effective brand communications possible often requires collaboration, which I relish. During my career I have worked with a wide range of skilled partners including architects, animators, web builders, directors, photographers, writers and editors.

Whether big or small, I approach all assignments with the same high level of enthusiasm and attention to detail. For me, it's all about the work.

WHAT HAS BEEN DIFFICULT FOR YOU AT THE BEGINNING?

There hasn't been too many difficulties so far. I do a mixture of my own studio projects and freelance work for other agencies, which means the best of both worlds. Working alone solves a lot of problems but also creates many more.

WHAT ROLES DO YOU PLAY IN THE FIRM?

It's currently a one-man studio so I do everything from initial client meetings, quoting through to concept, design and artwork.

HOW DO YOU PROMOTE YOURSELF?

I don't actively promote my services. I generally get commissions through word of mouth.

WHAT MAKE(S) SMALL STUDIOS SUSTAINABLE? WHAT IS MOST CRITICAL FOR STUDIOS LIKE YOURS TO GAIN A FOOTHOLD IN THE COMPETITIVE MARKET?

Small studios can react quicker, give a much more tailored personal solution and give the client direct contact and a discourse with creatives. This is an advantage both for the creative and the client. For the client it means less overheads with faster turn around. For me, direct client contact means a better understanding of their needs and a clear insight into the business firsthand.

02

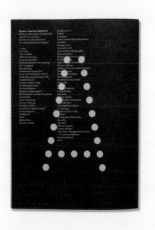

03

IT MIGHT BE EASIER FOR LARGE DESIGN AGENCIES TO WIN A JOB. WHAT ARE YOUR STRATEGIES TO BEAT THEM? HAVE YOU EVER LOST HAD TO GIVE UP AN OPPORTUNITY THAT MIGHT BE RELEVANT TO YOUR COMPANY SIZE?

Small studios definitely do not get considered for much larger jobs, however they do have more ability to take on smaller, more creatively fulfilling assignments.

WHAT ARE THE BEST AND WORST EXPERIENCES BY FAR?

Nearly all projects seem to have parts from both ends of the emotional spectrum. Still as they say in Holland "there is no shine without friction".

HAVE YOU EVER THOUGHT ABOUT ADDING (A) NEW PARTNER(S) OR HIRING STAFF? WHAT COULD BE A PROBLEM YOU HAVE EVER IMAGINED?

I have thought about it, but to date it has never eventuated.

WHAT DO YOU DO WHEN YOU GET BOGGED DOWN AT A JOB?

Go to the library, park, or a walk.

IF YOUR STUDIO HAS TO GROW BIG ONE DAY. WHAT WOULD BE THE ULTIMATE SIZE AND THE TRADITION(S) ETHOS TO KEEP?

Ten would be ideal. Big enough to be able to take on larger assignments but small enough not to take on work we don't want to do. The design ethos would have to stay. Quality of design output will always be at the forefront of what we do for clients.

04

05

06

07

08

"My ultimate aspiration would be overall art direction in multiple creative fields."

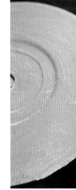

JORGE AMADOR

Porto, Portugal

. . . .

Key member / Jorge Amador
Specialties / Graphic design, Illustration
URL / www.majordogear.com

. . . .

Est. 2007

Portuguese-born Jorge Amador, alias majordogear, is a self-taught designer based in Porto, Portugal. His work is multi-disciplinary, revolving around graphic identity, illustrations, editorial and even product design, with a passionate and intuitive approach since he started his operation independently in 2007. His portfolio features collaborations with individuals and companies, including record labels and creative practices.

02

01

HOW DID YOU START YOUR COMPANY? WHAT IS/ARE YOUR CREED(S) AND ASPIRATION(S)?

After a couple of years working for companies and brands I had to consider searching for a job at other design studios. I've always had the feedback that people on the other side of the table liked the portfolio and its multidisciplinary aspect, and that they loved the idea of a self-taught creative mind. But the fact is that no one really takes the risk of hiring one, and if they do, it's for half the price and you're (forever) at the bottom of the chain.

Given this, I decided the best way I could get away with this was to do my own thing. So I focused on promoting my work, via web blogs, social networks, connections with friends, and friends of friends, or just straight up self-initiated projects with people I would like to work with and that could give me more exposure, and hopefully more work!

As for aspirations, I would say my ultimate aspiration would be overall art direction on multiple creative fields, from visual communication to music, video, woodworks, or who knows… culinary!

WHAT HAS BEEN DIFFICULT FOR YOU AT THE BEGINNING?

Well so far the difficult part really was the beginning, the kick-off and recognition, but that is slowly starting to pay. Currently the only difficulty is… taxes and more taxes!!!!

WHAT ROLES DO YOU PLAY IN THE FIRM?

In a way, I am "the firm", so I do it all!

HOW DO YOU PROMOTE YOURSELF?

Sometimes via web in an unaggressive way, but mostly through good relationships and word of mouth.

WHAT MAKE(S) SMALL STUDIOS SUSTAINABLE? WHAT IS MOST CRITICAL FOR STUDIOS LIKE YOURS TO GAIN A FOOTHOLD IN THE COMPETITIVE MARKET?

The first rule of running a small yet sustainable studio is: do not take a step bigger than your leg, go slowly but surely.

Second rule: keep your friends close, work with your friends if they are starting up something and if it looks good or smells good, help them, not necessarily for free but think service exchange. If they succeed you will thrive along.

The competition from bigger studios at the same price can be a stone at your feet, but it won't be competition at all if you handle it right, have your own niche in the market and establish your own style or approach to make you stand out. Somewhere out there, there's always a client that wants his problem solved in a particular way and not necessarily by the most renowned studio with the biggest name behind it!!

IT MIGHT BE EASIER FOR LARGE DESIGN AGENCIES TO WIN A JOB. WHAT ARE YOUR STRATEGIES TO BEAT THEM? HAVE YOU EVER LOST HAD TO GIVE UP AN OPPORTUNITY THAT MIGHT BE RELEVANT TO YOUR COMPANY SIZE?

I don't really try to beat them or tend to see them as competition. I've never had to say no to a "big brief" because of my "small size" but if such thing ever comes up, I won't give it up, per se. I'll redirect it to the proper place, maybe to a bigger studio of a friend, because when the time comes that friend will think the same way and redirect opportunities my way.

03

04

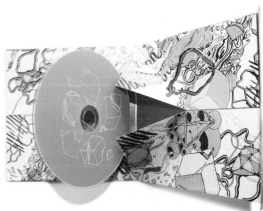

WHAT ARE THE BEST AND WORST EXPERIENCES BY FAR?

The best experience is when you open your e-mail and out of nowhere there's an invitation asking you to speak at some conference or to participate in a book or just a genuine interest in what you do. That always makes my day.

The worst experience is when the client has deeply preconceived ideas of what he wants and how he wants it, and what he thinks is utterly right and wrong and generally knows better than you and starts to assume that your choices are not the best because of "how the public perceives it". Basically a client that underestimates the intelligence of the public. Ultimately you get this feeling that he doesn't know why he needs a designer, or what a designer's part really is, to begin with.

HAVE YOU EVER THOUGHT ABOUT ADDING (A) NEW PARTNER(S) OR HIRING STAFF? WHAT COULD BE A PROBLEM YOU HAVE EVER IMAGINED?

I've thought about it many times, more like an equal partner or partners, but so far everyone I've ever wanted to work with is doing their own thing, so I guess I'll wait.

It has to be the right person, preferably a friend that knows me. I tend to try to control everything, this can be a problem if the person I'm working with doesn't know me well enough to say "hey... f*ck off!"

05

MAJOR DOGEAR

M A JR

G R D M

G E B A R

06

07

08

WHAT DO YOU DO WHEN YOU GET BOGGED DOWN AT A JOB?

I try to shut myself off from the project or even from design itself. Go for a jog, play some music or just fill myself with good food (cooked by me) and empty my brain with a good sleep.

DO YOU INTEND TO RETAIN YOUR PRACTICE'S CURRENT SIZE? IF IT HAS TO GROW BIG ONE DAY, WHAT WOULD BE THE ULTIMATE SIZE AND THE TRADITION(S) ETHOS TO KEEP?

Eventually I would like to create a kind of design lab-lounge open to the public, some place where people could come in, have the time, take a seat, a drink or something, enjoy the space while there is a work flow happening at the same time. But no bigger than two or three persons (not necessarily designers).

I rather keep it small but if it has to go big, it has to focus on the work for friends only or with projects I identify myself with and never have to accept a boring or uninteresting brief because of financial needs. Quite the dream I'm having now!

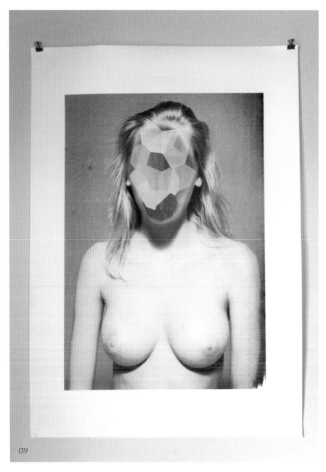

09

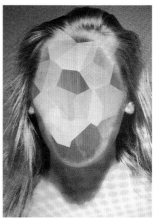

10

11

01 / Latin Love_2010
Limited wall piece interpreting "love".

02 / Design & Art Sale_2010
Flyer for a series of flash sales.

03 / Lost Gorbachevs+Tinnitus: Split_2012
Record packaging with artwork.

04 / 28//03//2012_2012
Illustration and EP packaging for Amador's
personal music project.

05 / White Studio – Window_2012
Installation on the theme of "Portugal from a
positive point of view".

06 / majordogear Identity_2011
Amador's business card with an anagram
formed from "Jorge Amador".

07 / Les Petits Riens Collectibles_2010
Merchandise for Dixit Design Lab.

08 / Feira de Edição Independente_2012
Collateral for Independent Publishing Fair.

09 / Silkscreen Experiments_2009
Screenprints exploring halftone frequencies,
paint opacity and gradients. B&W photo by
Ryan Mcginley.

10 / This is a Book About Planking_2011
Self-initiated illustration zine.

11 / CUBO Magazine_2011
Branding for a magazine focusing on ludic
events in Porto.

Portraits & studio shots: Sarah Skinner

"Experiment new possibilities for my design and more importantly not to do something twice."

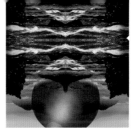

LESLIE DAVID
Paris, France

. . . .

Key member / Leslie David
Specialties / Art direction, Graphic design
URL / www.leslie-david.com

. . . .

Est. 2008

Born to creative parents who run a poster
business, Leslie David saw herself as a
freelancer quite early on, during her studies
at Ecole des Arts Decoratifs in Strasbourg,
where she started taking illustration jobs
for magazines and later joined petronio
associates as a junior art director in 2006.
Currently an independent art director,
graphic designer and illustrator, David's goal
is to broaden her creative experience
clients from diverse fields.

HOW DID YOU START YOUR COMPANY? WHAT IS/ARE YOUR CREED(S) AND ASPIRATION(S)?

I started working as a freelance when I was still a student. I was doing illustrations for magazines and newspapers. This was a way to earn money and build my portfolio at the same time, which is more profitable than working as a waitress! (well, ok I did that too back then...) While I was looking for an internship, a big shot agency offered me a position as junior art director. I could not turn it down. I stayed there for two years, but I knew that it was just a first step before working as a freelance, which was my aspiration. I could not conceive of having a boss and strict office hours! I quit one day when I could not take it anymore. I was really in need of space to breath and to make my own things. Being a freelance was my way to nurture my creative identity and also express all the ideas I had been holding back for two years.

I don't have a design philosophy or creative guideline per se. My aim is to enjoy and have fun while I'm working. I like to experiment new possibilities for my design and more importantly I try not to do something twice.

WHAT HAS BEEN DIFFICULT FOR YOU AT THE BEGINNING?

At the start it was a little bit frightening to wait for calls, but I was lucky to have the network that I started building when I was at school.

WHAT ROLES DO YOU PLAY IN THE FIRM?

From the beginning I was running the studio by myself but recently I took a step forward and decided to work with a studio manager and a design intern. Being three make the process smoother!

HOW DO YOU PROMOTE YOURSELF?

I regularly update my website and my Facebook page, with news and projects. I'm not really good with Twitter. There aren't enough [space for] pictures! I also send newsletters on a regular basis and try to keep in touch as much as possible with my clients.

WHAT MAKE(S) SMALL STUDIOS SUSTAINABLE? WHAT IS MOST CRITICAL FOR STUDIOS LIKE YOURS TO GAIN A FOOTHOLD IN THE COMPETITIVE MARKET?

To me, the studio size coincides with the projects' size. For more substantial projects (budget- and concept-wise), clients tend to trust and work with bigger studios or agencies, which is a pity but logical in a way...

IT MIGHT BE EASIER FOR LARGE DESIGN AGENCIES TO WIN A JOB. WHAT ARE YOUR STRATEGIES TO BEAT THEM? HAVE YOU EVER LOST HAD TO GIVE UP AN OPPORTUNITY THAT MIGHT BE RELEVANT TO YOUR COMPANY SIZE?

As a small-scale graphic design studio, we are not looking to compete with bigger agencies. As mentioned before, to us, the size of the project must somehow coincide with the studio agency size and capacities. We are sometimes contacted by clients, amongst other agencies, which lead to different proposals and approaches, both for the design and the client relationship. In the end we have our arguments and agencies have theirs. So we do not really feel the competition.

02

03

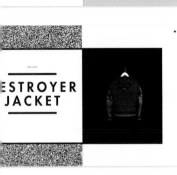

ESTROYER
JACKET

questions
réponses

OUR
CHOSEN
ONES

THE
LAST
STRAW

STADIUM
PARIS

STADIUM
PARIS

STADIUM
PARIS

STADIUM
PARIS

ALWAYS
ON THE
RUN

WHAT ARE THE BEST AND WORST EXPERIENCES BY FAR?

The worst experience was working in an agency. The best experience is by far to be free. Free to choose my projects and decide how I drive them. It is a real luxury that I would never give up on.

HAVE YOU EVER THOUGHT ABOUT ADDING (A) NEW PARTNER(S) OR HIRING STAFF? WHAT COULD BE A PROBLEM YOU HAVE EVER IMAGINED?

Yes indeed and I decided to take it to the next level this year.

I now work with a studio manager who is in charge of everything not design-related and I'm really happy about it.

Another step would be to have a full-time designer with whom I could share workload with. This is not happening yet but hopefully in the near future!

WHAT DO YOU DO WHEN YOU GET BOGGED DOWN AT A JOB?

I switch to another project, sleep on it and then come back to it the next day.

DO YOU INTEND TO RETAIN YOUR PRACTICE'S CURRENT SIZE? IF IT HAS TO GROW BIG ONE DAY, WHAT WOULD BE THE ULTIMATE SIZE?

Yes. I thought about it and I know that a big studio is not what I'm heading towards, mostly because it would necessarily reduce my design time. I would prefer a team of four to five to keep it personal and balanced between design and management.

AND THE TRADITION(S) ETHOS TO KEEP?

It would be the tradition to have birthday and Christmas parties!

04

05

06

07

08

01 / *Marc Riboud Exhibition_2011*
Photo exhibition identity and collateral.

02 / *Chalayan Airborne_2011*
Packaging for a fragrance introduced by
Chalayan and Comme des Garçons.

03 / *Surface to Air_2011*
Print for Surface to Air's S/S collection.

04 / *Stadium Paris_2011*
Identity, layout and art direction for Nike
Magazine.

05 / *Painting Please!_2011*
Illustrations made to celebrate Please!
magazine's 5th birthday. Pictures by
Nagi Sakai.

06 / *Souvenirs de Paris_2011*
Postcard set for colette.

07 / *Maison Michel S/S 12 Lookbook_2011*
Art direcion for a hatmaker's lookbook.

08 / *Andrea Crews Scarfs_2010*
Silk scarves print and packaging for Andrea Crews' fall collection.

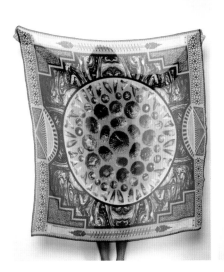

> "I'm not a man of faith so I really don't have more creed than my Internet connection, as I am."

PAUERR
Barcelona, Spain

. . . .

Key member / Pau Garcia Sanchez
Specialties / Graphic design, Movies
URL / www.pauerr.com

. . . .

Est. 2010

Pau Garcia Sanchez (b.1989) calls himself a "freak designer" and "poetic copywriter". Starting off with corporate identity design on a dare, Sanchez moves on to create with a range of media, including graphics, physical crafts and motion pictures, to realise his whimsy views in self-initiated projects as well as commissioned works. Sanchez is also a co-founder of Arbusto films.

I HAVE
BEEN
UNDER
THE RAIN
FOR
SIX
HOURS

I HAVE BEEN SERIES

01

HOW DID YOU START YOUR COMPANY? WHAT IS/ARE YOUR CREED(S) AND ASPIRATION(S)?

I started Pauerr Design around 2010. Some friends challenged me to create a corporate identity for a pornographic film studio. I made it. After this crazy brand I start receiving lots of different jobs (not related to the sex world. Well... not at all). I'm not a man of faith so I really don't have more creed than my Internet connection, as I am.

WHAT HAS BEEN DIFFICULT FOR YOU AT THE BEGINNING?

The most difficult thing to do when I start my practice is to be conscious of whether you are doing a good job or a mess. Most of the time you are making decisions on your own and you have to be really clever to learn from your errors.

WHAT ROLES DO YOU PLAY IN THE FIRM?

I try to be auto self-sufficient ninety percent of the time. I'm kind of an "orchestra-man". You can see me working as a programmer, copywriter, motion graphic designer or graphic designer.

HOW DO YOU PROMOTE YOURSELF?

Well, that's a good question. After lots of attempts I had a formula that always has repercussions — do something free for yourself, something that you really enjoy. That is the best promotion you can have. You are showing your best and what you want to do. That way is easier to get a project that is near your line of work.

WHAT MAKE(S) SMALL STUDIOS SUSTAINABLE? WHAT IS MOST CRITICAL FOR STUDIOS LIKE YOURS TO GAIN A FOOTHOLD IN THE COMPETITIVE MARKET?

It's a weird mix between hard work, luck and networking. The most critical thing is to have good and regular clients. I think that, to get a job done well, there has to be a kind of amorousness between you and your client. But it is not easy to fall in love with a client. They normally are fat.

IT MIGHT BE EASIER FOR LARGE DESIGN AGENCIES TO WIN A JOB. WHAT ARE YOUR STRATEGIES TO BEAT THEM? HAVE YOU EVER LOST HAD TO GIVE UP AN OPPORTUNITY THAT MIGHT BE RELEVANT TO YOUR COMPANY SIZE?

That's not true at all. After working in some big agencies, I know at first hand that a big company is synonymous with chaos and impersonal treatment. Just play this point to your advantage, and then if you can afford it, do all the work and use your network.

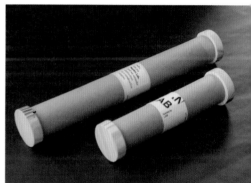

WHAT ARE THE BEST AND WORST EXPERIENCES BY FAR?

My best experience has been realising Nankin Lab, an experimental design laboratory, from the outline to the final arts, from the chaos of a weird idea to a very specific project. For me it is not the best but the most complete project I have ever done. My worst experience was with an American client whom I had been working for more than a month non-stop in the production of a brand and disappeared midway. You know dark holes? The unexpected ones abducted my client. I had set aside my own work, my family and my friends to do this project for finally nothing.

HAVE YOU EVER THOUGHT ABOUT ADDING (A) NEW PARTNER(S) OR HIRING STAFF? WHAT COULD BE A PROBLEM YOU HAVE EVER IMAGINED?

Not until now. Well, the problem is obvious. If you start working with somebody and unexpectedly [things] do not work out, you will have to fire that somebody. Nobody likes to fire anybody, not me for sure. And actually I have always been able to manage all the work I have in hand.

WHAT DO YOU DO WHEN YOU GET BOGGED DOWN AT A JOB?

Walk. It really works. Go to the street and walk. It's really silly but it always works. Well, I suppose that if you are in a little village in the middle of nowhere it could be difficult but I think that sticking to the screen all day is not good for our creative paths.

DO YOU INTEND TO RETAIN YOUR PRACTICE'S CURRENT SIZE? IF IT HAS TO GROW BIG ONE DAY, WHAT WOULD BE THE ULTIMATE SIZE?

Sure. Actually I don't want to grow, not as a company, not in project. I love to have my time to develop my own projects. Creating you own projects will make your professional projects better.

AND THE TRADITION(S) ETHOS TO KEEP?

Friday morning yoga.

03

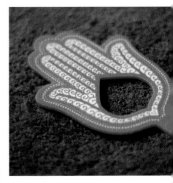

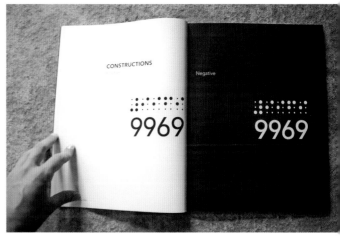

04

01 / I Have Been Series_2012
Experimental posters. Produced with Pol
Trias and Rodney Bunker.

02 / Nankin Lab_2012
Identity for an experimental design
studio. Produced with Pol Trias.

03 / The Buddhist Flyswatter_2012
Prototype flyswatter which never kills.
Produced with Clara Romani.

04 / 9969_2011
Identity for an enterprise who works with
the visually-impaired. Produced with
Eva Vera.

SAM FLAHERTY CREATIVE

London, UK

. . . .

👤 🇬🇧

Key member / Sam Flaherty
Specialties / Art direction, Graphic design
URL / www.samflahertycreative.com

. . . .

Est. 2009

Sam Flaherty is a graphic designer and art director currently based in London. Having worked at creative agencies and on various magazines in New Zealand and Australia for the last five years. Flaherty believes in creating clear, concise messages through design elegance and reduction. His focuses are typography, graphic identity and editorial design. He has worked with a broad range of clients, extending from the likes of fashion blogs, photographers, and musicians to top international brands.

"It's important to find your creative voice by yourself first, and not rush into a relationship."

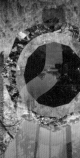

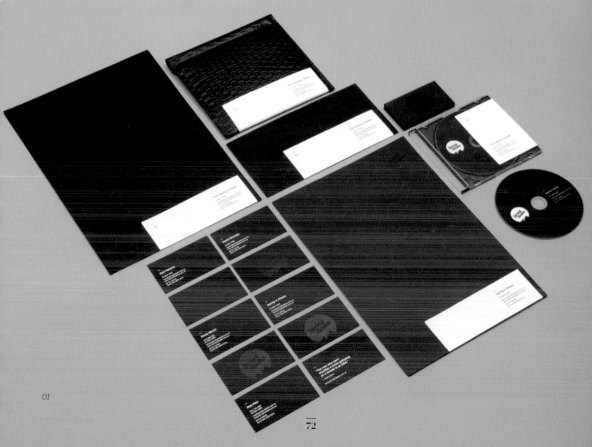

HOW DID YOU START YOUR COMPANY? WHAT IS ARE YOUR CREED(S) AND ASPIRATION(S)?

I started working as a freelance designer when I got involved with *Fluro magazine* back in 2008 — I ended up working for clients out of the magazine's office. I think from the start my aspiration has been to enjoy the freedom that a creative lifestyle affords. Not many careers offer the same amount of variety as ours — we are the lucky ones.

WHAT HAS BEEN DIFFICULT FOR YOU AT THE BEGINNING?

It's always a risk going out on your own, but I think it can snowball relatively quickly.

WHAT ROLES DO YOU PLAY IN THE FIRM?

Well, it's actually just me — so I do everything! That is, unless I'm working with another freelancer or studio on a project, or bring somebody onto a project myself.

HOW DO YOU PROMOTE YOURSELF?

There are a number of great websites around the world where are good to have a profile, and clients can find you from there. Also, word of mouth is a big one. Once you do some work for a client, they tend to tell others — especially if you do a good job.

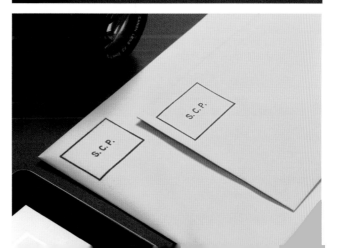

03

04

WHAT MAKE(S) SMALL STUDIOS SUSTAINABLE? WHAT IS MOST CRITICAL FOR STUDIOS LIKE YOURS TO GAIN A FOOTHOLD IN THE COMPETITIVE MARKET?

Small studios simply don't have the overheads. We can easily adjust our team size on a project basis. I would say that smaller teams can also deliver projects without clutter — we can really listen to our clients and deal with them directly, which is something you don't often find in the larger agencies.

IT MIGHT BE EASIER FOR LARGE DESIGN AGENCIES TO WIN A JOB. WHAT ARE YOUR STRATEGIES TO BEAT THEM? HAVE YOU EVER LOST HAD TO GIVE UP AN OPPORTUNITY THAT MIGHT BE RELEVANT TO YOUR COMPANY SIZE?

I think that small studios can pack a powerful punch when it comes to pitching — larger agencies can sometimes become complacent at this stage. Having said that, it can certainly be daunting when you come up against a large agency! The smaller studios just need to explain to the client the benefits of working with a small team.

WHAT ARE THE BEST AND WORST EXPERIENCES BY FAR?

The best experiences are always completing a job that you can be proud of. Getting a magazine back from the printers, visiting a new website that's gone live or seeing a brand that you've created out in the marketplace — those are the reasons we do what we do. In terms of my worst experience, it's always heart-stopping when you find a typo!

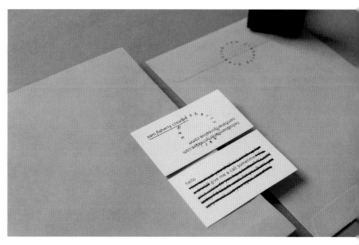

HAVE YOU EVER THOUGHT ABOUT ADDING (A) NEW PARTNER(S) OR HIRING STAFF? WHAT COULD BE A PROBLEM YOU HAVE EVER IMAGINED?

I'd say that when the time is right, I will end up working alongside a partner. I think it's important to find your creative voice by yourself first, and not rush into a relationship.

WHAT DO YOU DO WHEN YOU GET BOGGED DOWN AT A JOB?

A long walk through the park usually cures all. Flick through some magazines and books, visit some creative blogs, and above all don't panic — problems are created to be solved.

IF YOUR STUDIO HAS TO GROW BIG ONE DAY, WHAT WOULD BE THE ULTIMATE SIZE AND THE TRADITION(S) ETHOS TO KEEP?

I'm a fan of small studios, so I would say that five or six is a fairly good number. Above all, I'd want to retain that sense of freedom, independence and fun.

06

01 / *Spring In Alaska_2011-12*
Brand revamp during employment at the multidisciplinary creative agency.

02 / *Sam Conaglen_2010*
Identity for a photographer.

03 / *Pulp Magazine_2011*
Redesign for a seminal cultural magazine in New Zealand.

04 / *You Are Not Alone_2010*
Collateral for an exhibition held in Wellington, New Zealand.

05 / *Sam Flaherty Creative_2012*
Personal branding and identity.

06 / *Henry Godzilla_2012*
Fashion label branding.

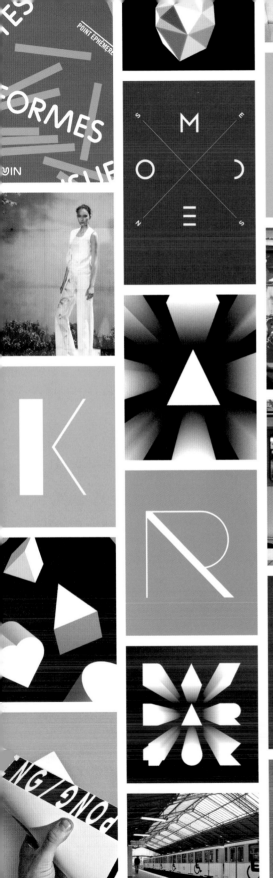

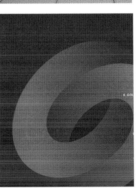

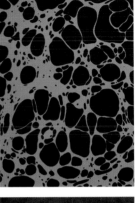

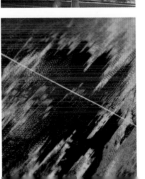

"It actually seemed like the obvious next step. I never really questioned this choice."

STUDIO FREDERIC TACER
Paris, France

....

Key member / Frederic Tacer
Specialties / Art direction, Graphic design
URL / www.frederictacer.net

....

Est. 2010

Frederic Tacer is an independent French art director and graphic designer born in 1985. After graduating with highest honours from the National College of Arts and Design in Paris and working as an in-house designer for the Institute of Contemporary Arts in London. he founded his studio in Paris in 2010, providing print and editorial design solutions defined by a focus on typographic and structural details. Tacer's work is visible in both cultural and commercial realms.

MAY
UNE 2

01

HOW DID YOU START YOUR COMPANY? WHAT IS/ARE YOUR CREED(S) AND ASPIRATION(S)?

I founded my studio at the beginning of 2010, right after coming back from London and only a year and a half after my graduation. I had a few projects in hand and felt prepared. It actually seemed like the obvious next step. I never really questioned this choice.

Graphic design has always been a passion more than a job to me. That's why my creed is to never stop having fun with what I do. The day I won't be happy to go to work anymore will be the sign that I need to quit and do something else. The notion of challenge and constant exploration are also primordial to my practice. I can't stand doing the same thing twice otherwise I will feel like I'm wasting time.

WHAT HAS BEEN DIFFICULT FOR YOU AT THE BEGINNING?

It must have been the paperwork. I still don't feel — and probably will never feel — comfortable with that aspect of the job because that actually reminds me that it is a job.

WHAT ROLES DO YOU PLAY IN THE FIRM?

As I work by myself most of the time, I can have a lot of various roles to play. It is sometimes exhausting — yes, and it could sound like I'm complaining — but this versatility is actually what I like the most about my job. The best side of it is that I always know who to blame when there's the slightest problem — myself. But I never hesitate to collaborate with other people when a project requires it or when a task reaches my limits.

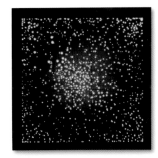

02

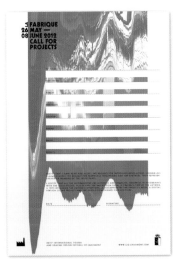

03

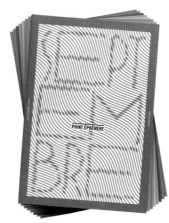

04

HOW DO YOU PROMOTE YOURSELF?

I try to update my website with recent works as frequently as possible and have a semblance of activity on social networks to keep followers posted, but that's not really my area of expertise. Most of the projects I work on come by word of mouth.

WHAT MAKE(S) SMALL STUDIOS SUSTAINABLE? WHAT IS MOST CRITICAL FOR STUDIOS LIKE YOURS TO GAIN A FOOTHOLD IN THE COMPETITIVE MARKET?

The reason why I used my own name for the studio is because I think it is important for people to know who they are dealing with. For instance, as part of my process, I always try to meet the persons I'm going to work with before starting a new project. I see myself more as an artisan than as a firm. And, in terms of design, I believe it is always more fruitful when a one-to-one relationship is established. That is what I think makes small studios valuable and necessary.

Now I suppose some clients might think a small structure would be less efficient than a big agency, and some might simply like the idea of having dozens of people working for them. I tend to think the more steps and people involved, the less pure will be the final result.

IT MIGHT BE EASIER FOR LARGE DESIGN AGENCIES TO WIN A JOB. WHAT ARE YOUR STRATEGIES TO BEAT THEM? HAVE YOU EVER LOST HAD TO GIVE UP AN OPPORTUNITY THAT MIGHT BE RELEVANT TO YOUR COMPANY SIZE?

I'm not sure whether it is easier for large companies to win a job. It all depends on the job and, most importantly, on the client. Anyhow, I've never had to give up that kind of opportunity so far. Moreover, I'm not really comfortable with the idea of competition. I, therefore, have no particular "strategy" (I always find the use of such a belligerent vocabulary a bit odd). I like to think that my work speaks for itself. I prefer that a client comes to me because he happened to come across my work and enjoyed it. It is much more rewarding than having to prove yourself by "defeating random opponents".

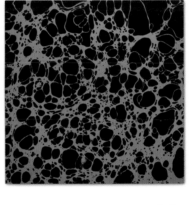

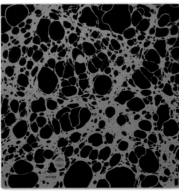

05

06

07

08

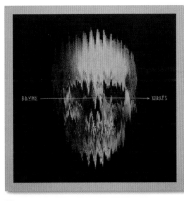

09

WHAT ARE THE BEST AND WORST EXPERIENCES BY FAR?

So far, my best experience must be the opportunity I've been given to work for Point Éphémère, an independent Parisian cultural centre with a concert hall, exhibition space, a bar-restaurant and artist-in-residency program. Since I moved to Paris for my studies, it has always been one of my favourite places to hang out. It's perfect to have a drink on sunny days (it opens on the canal Saint-Martin) and it offers a top-notch musical programming in a cosy venue. I remember myself, as a student (and a music lover), thinking I would be the happiest graphic designer if I could work for such a place. Plus, I have access to all the gigs now! Between this and the various record sleeves I work on now, I feel like I've made one of my dreams as a boy come true.

As for the worst experience, it was probably realising that some people just don't respect your work and can abuse your kindness. Being at the end of the "production line" can sometimes be ungrateful. Fortunately, it is pretty rare.

HAVE YOU EVER THOUGHT ABOUT ADDING (A) NEW PARTNER(S) OR HIRING STAFF? WHAT COULD BE A PROBLEM YOU HAVE EVER IMAGINED?

I'm perpetually questioning my practice, whether it's my graphic choices on a project or my work process. I, therefore, sometimes think about adding staff or partner, of course. However, it is not only a matter of will but also of feeling. I occasionally work with some friends on several projects but the truth is that I've never yet met *the* partner whom I feel like working with all day long. To make it interesting, you do not only have to find someone you get along with but who is also able to challenge your vision and choices in a constructive manner. I think it's a subtle balance that is not so easy to find. So I don't exclude this option but it's not really an issue right now. I suppose as long as I can manage the amount of work I'm given, the studio size will remain the same.

11

WHAT DO YOU DO WHEN YOU GET BOGGED DOWN AT A JOB?

Music has always been a great source of inspiration to me. I listen to a lot of music while I work. It stimulates my creativity. But when I'm really stuck on a problem, the best way to solve it is to try and look at it with fresh eyes. That's why, most of the time, I clear my mind with things that have nothing to do with graphic design or the projects on which I'm working. A drink with friends, a good meal, a concert, a book, an exhibition, a movie… many things work.

DO YOU INTEND TO RETAIN YOUR PRACTICE'S CURRENT SIZE? IF IT HAS TO GROW BIG ONE DAY, WHAT WOULD BE THE ULTIMATE SIZE?

When it comes to work, I know I can be a control freak. I find it hard to delegate. I need to "get my hands dirty". I could never sell to a client an idea I haven't worked on — it wouldn't feel legitimate to me. Moreover, I take absolutely no pleasure in giving orders or managing a team. I don't consider design as a business but as a craft. Hence the smaller, the better.

AND THE TRADITION(S) ETHOS TO KEEP?

Never stop having fun; never have the feeling that you're doing something because you have to; never think "good enough" is good enough; never stop trying to make things simpler.

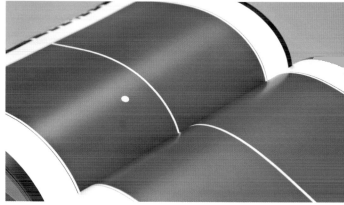

12

01 / Petites Formes (D)cousues_2011-12
Posters and identity for a contemporary dance festival.

02 / Silane: Stars_2010
Record sleeve design.

03 / La Fabrique_2012
Posters for the third edition of La Fabrique during the International Graphic Design Festival of Chaumont.

04, 09 / Point Éphémère Monthly Guide_2011-12
Monthly publication for Parisian cultural centre and venue, Point Éphémère.

05 / Apes Did Ensemble_2010
Record sleeve design.

06 / Frog_2012
Record sleeve design.

07 / Takaaaki_2011
Record packaging for a dupstep artist.

08 / Mode & Sens_2011
Identity for EnsAD's fashion show. Art directed by Clarita Spindler. Photos by Olivia Fremineau.

10 / Xerxès_2012
Record sleeve design.

11 / PING/PONG_2012
A palindromic book for an interactive reading experience.

12 / Unknown Pleasures_2011
Self-initiated art project as a tribute to Joy Division and Peter Saville.

SO
10

SO10 · 2UO · 3RIO
Small Studio · Great Impact

First published and distributed by
viction:workshop ltd.

viction:ary™

viction:workshop ltd.
Unit C, 7/F, Seabright Plaza, 9-23 Shell Street,
North Point, Hong Kong
Url: www.victionary.com   Email: we@victionary.com
f www.facebook.com/victionworkshop
🐦 www.twitter.com/victionary_
🐙 www.weibo.com/victionary

Edited and produced by viction:ary

Concepts & art direction by Victor Cheung
Book design by viction:workshop ltd.
Cover image on slipcase by Designbolaget

ISBN 978-988-19439-1-0

Printed and bound in China

Acknowledgements

We would like to thank all the designers and companies who have involved in
the production of this book. This project would not have been accomplished
without their significant contribution to the compilation of this book. We would
also like to express our gratitude to all the producers for their invaluable
opinions and assistance throughout this entire project. The successful
completion also owes a great deal to many professionals in the creative
industry who have given us precious insights and comments. And to the many
others whose names are not credited but have made specific input in this
book, we thank you for your continuous support the whole time.

Future Editions

If you wish to participate in viction:ary's future projects and publications,
please send your website or portfolio to submit@victionary.com